First published in Great Britain in 2023 by Farshore
An imprint of HarperCollins*Publishers*
1 London Bridge Street, London SE1 9GF
www.farshore.co.uk

HarperCollins*Publishers*
Macken House, 39/40 Mayor Street Upper,
Dublin 1, D01 C9W8, Ireland

Written by Laura Jackson

ISBN 978 0 00 853717 3
Printed in Romania
001

A CIP catalogue record for this title is available from the British Library.

Parental guidance is advised for all craft and colouring activities.
Always ask an adult to help when using glue, paint and scissors.
Wear protective clothing and cover surfaces to avoid staining.

Stay safe online. Farshore is not responsible
for content hosted by third parties.

Farshore takes its responsibility to the planet and its inhabitants very seriously.
We aim to use papers from well-managed forests run by responsible suppliers.

This
Disney Princess
Annual 2024 belongs to

....

....

Age ....

Disney

PRINCESS

Annual 2024

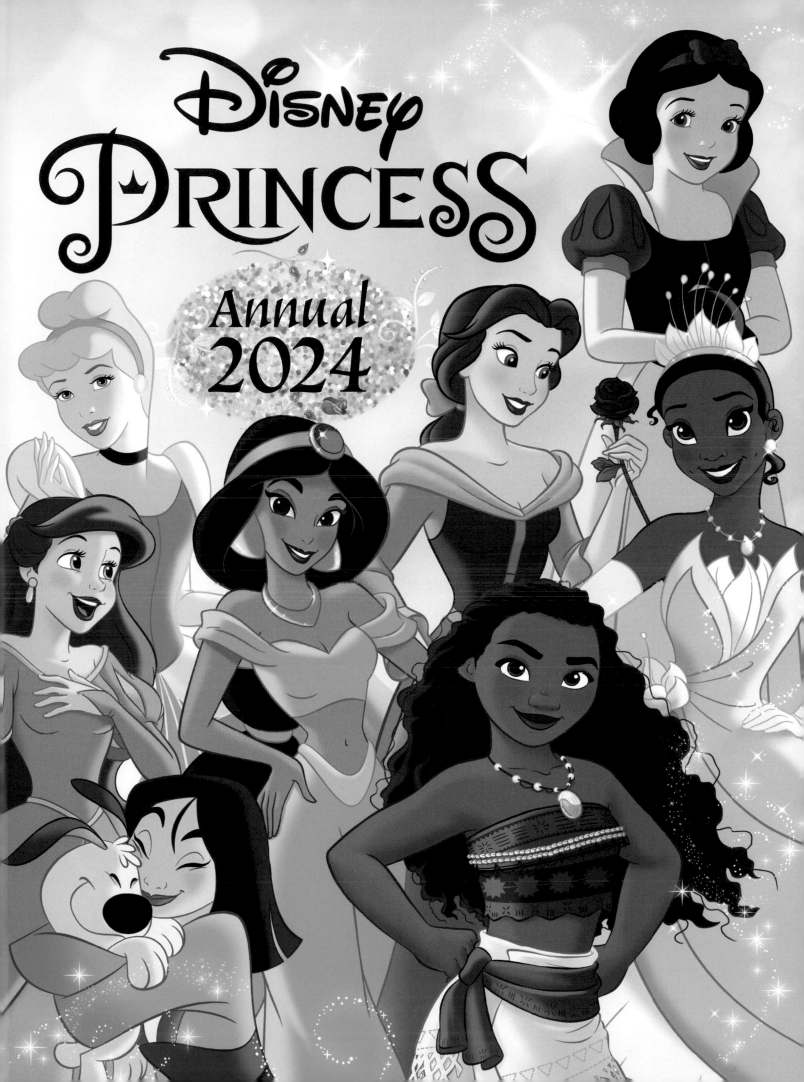

What's Inside?

Curious Ariel

Best friend ...
Flounder.

Likes ...
to sing and explore.

Collects ...
human treasures
from sunken ships.

Princess power ...
Ariel saved Prince
Eric from drowning.

Ariel's story ...
Ariel dreams of adventures above the sea. But when she does a dangerous deal with a sea witch to visit the human world, her life is turned on its fin. Luckily, with a little help from her friends and the magic of true love, Ariel's dreams might all just come true ...

Isn't it fantastic?

A Wonderful World

Ariel is excited to explore the world above the waves. A snowy adventure awaits!

Can you spot these close-ups in the big picture? Tick ✔ each one when you spot it.

Answers on page 69.

Splashy Quiz

Life under the sea and on land is full of fun, friendship and surprises. Take this quiz all about Ariel and the people and creatures in her world.

1

Point to the SMALLEST friend.

a

b

c

d

2

Point to the BIGGEST friend (or enemy)!

a

b

c

d

3

Point to two people in Ariel's FAMILY.

a

b

c

d

4

Point to Ariel wearing a BLUE dress.

a

b

c

d

Best Friends

Whoosh! Ursula has cast a spell and Flounder is stuck in a bubble. Help guide Ariel safely through the water to rescue her best friend.

← START

← FINISH

Answers on page 69.

The Big Race

1 Ariel and Flounder were very busy. The kingdom's annual Great Chariot Race was coming up and the friends were putting the finishing touches to Ariel's chariot.

It looks great!

Out of my way everyone!

1 Circle the sea creature pulling Ariel's chariot.

a

b

2 Suddenly, a ginormous chariot pulled by 10 strong eels appeared. Its driver was wearing a veil which hid their face. The driver looked at Ariel's chariot and laughed cruelly.

See you at the race, losers!

3 "You'll never win the race with that pathetic little thing!" the eels cried, before racing off, leaving Ariel and Flounder bobbing up and down in their wake. "Who was that?" Ariel wondered.

On your marks, get set, go!

4 The day of the race soon arrived. As Ariel lined up at the start, she saw the veiled driver who sneered at her. Then, King Triton banged two shells together and the contestants were off.

2 Spot these chariots at the starting line.

a

b

c

Hey, that's not fair!

5 The veiled driver took the lead with Ariel following close behind, but then the eels started playing dirty. First they weaved from side to side to make the water choppy.

6 Then they threw seaweed in Ariel's path so her seahorses got tangled up. Finally, they squirted squid ink into the water so that Ariel couldn't see where she was going.

Ariel overcame each problem, but got further behind. A little way down the track, she was surprised to see the veiled driver's chariot stuck in some weeds. And their veil had come undone ...

It's you!

8 "Ursula!" Ariel gasped, as she realised it was the sea witch. "Daddy banished you from the Kingdom." "And that's why I wanted to beat his daughter in this race!" Ursula cried, angrily.

She didn't even say 'thank you'!

9 Ariel was too kind to leave Ursula stranded so she asked some crab friends to cut her free. "I'll get my own back soon!" Ursula cried furiously, as she swam away.

 3 Count the helpful crabs.

10 Ariel was the last contestant to cross the finish line but she didn't mind. "I did the right thing helping Ursula and that's all that matters," she told Flounder.

11 "And now we have a whole year to make the best chariot this kingdom has ever seen! If Ursula shows up again next time, we'll be ready for her!"

4 Find 5 orange fish in the picture.

5 Draw a chariot for Ariel to race in next time.

All About ...
Clever Belle

Likes ...
to read books and meet new people.

Dreams ...
of adventures outside her small town.

Princess power ...
Belle bravely helped the Beast when nobody else would.

Belle's story ...
Belle finds magic in books. She spends so much time reading, the people in her town don't always understand her. Not that Belle minds! She likes being true to herself, and to others. So when people turn on the Beast, she is ready to risk everything to stick up for what is right.

Beauty is found within.

Sparkly Designs

It's time to shine! Transform Belle's party dress into something wonderful. Add colours, patterns and fun accessories.

Belle has brought a present for the Beast. Draw what you think it is.

Magical Memory

Sparkling snow is falling everywhere! Can you spot 5 snowy differences in picture 2?

Trace around one part of this snowman each time you find a difference.

1

2

18

Answers on page 69.

Starry Surprise

It's dark at the castle and the stars are shining bright. Belle and her friends have come outside to play a game of hide and seek. Can you match up each friend to their shadow?

Belle's Busy Day

Trace the time on the clocks, follow the yellow finger trail and do the challenges as you join Belle on her busy day.

7 o'clock

Rise and shine! Draw some yummy food for Belle's breakfast.

11 o'clock

Tell Belle all about your favourite book.

1 o'clock

Let's race! Make a clip-clop sound, just like Phillippe.

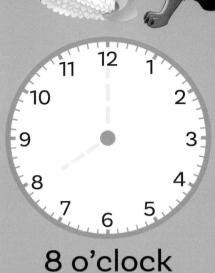

4 o'clock

Say 'hello' to Maurice! Then draw a tasty treat for him to eat.

8 o'clock

Let's dance! Twirl gracefully around the room just like Belle and the Beast.

9 o'clock

Goodnight Belle! How many stars can you count?

I count ☐ stars.

Answers on page 69.

All About...
Fun Rapunzel

Best friend ...
Pascal the chameleon.

Likes ...
to paint and play music.

Dislikes ...
wearing shoes!

Princess power ...
Rapunzel never gives up hope.

Rapunzel's story ...
Locked in a tower by Mother Gothel, Rapunzel is taught to fear the outside world. But when she sees floating lights in the sky, she just knows there is something good out there. With the help of her new friend Flynn Ryder, Rapunzel takes a risk and follows her dreams.

Dream free!

22

Get Your Sparkle On

Let's give Rapunzel's Christmas tree some serious sparkle. Grab your crayons and doodle glitter balls, twinkling lights and dazzling baubles.

Draw some presents under her tree.

Double Trouble

1 One day, Rapunzel was in her tower putting the finishing touches to a painting. She was really pleased with how it looked. "I think I'll hang this one up," she thought to herself.

Almost done.

 Circle what Rapunzel is painting.

 a

 b

 c

2 Suddenly Pascal appeared. Quick as a flash, the chameleon swung his tail and knocked a jar of water all over Rapunzel's picture, on purpose. "It's ruined!" she gasped in shock.

Why did you do that?

3 Rapunzel knew this kind of behaviour wasn't like Pascal at all. She tried to talk to her friend to find out what was wrong, but Pascal just ran away.

What's got into you today?

4

A little while later, Rapunzel was baking a cake. But as she picked up an egg, Pascal appeared and batted it onto the floor. It cracked open. "That was the last one," Rapunzel sighed.

5

Rapunzel decided to read her favourite book instead. But just as she was getting to the best bit, Pascal jumped up onto the windowsill and knocked the book out of the open window.

2 Decorate this cupcake for Rapunzel.

PASCAL!

6

"Why are you being so naughty?" Rapunzel asked in despair. Just then, she heard a noise and turned around to see Pascal climbing through the window with a flower in his mouth.

25

7 How could Pascal be there when he was behind her a moment ago? Suddenly Rapunzel realised there were two chameleons and only one of them was the real Pascal.

You're not Pascal!

8 "So it wasn't you being naughty," Rapunzel said, as Pascal gave her the flower he'd picked. "You weren't even here. You were out in the forest picking this for me."

Thank you for my flower.

3 Find a difference between these 2 pictures of the real Pascal.

a

b

Answer on page 69.

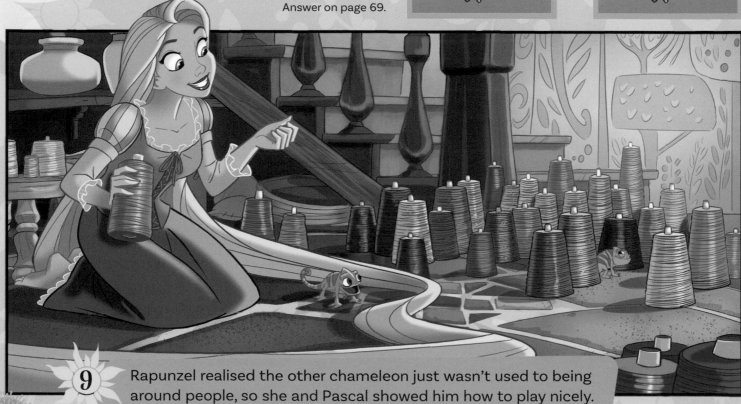

9 Rapunzel realised the other chameleon just wasn't used to being around people, so she and Pascal showed him how to play nicely. The three of them had a lovely afternoon together.

10 Later, as it was getting dark, the other chameleon turned to Rapunzel and Pascal as if to say goodbye, then climbed out of the window and down the tower to the ground.

I'm glad you're such a well behaved chameleon!

11 Rapunzel smiled as they saw their new friend join a group of chameleons and disappear into the forest. "He has his family and I have mine," she said, hugging Pascal tightly.

The End

4 Spot this flying bird in the picture.

5 Draw your favourite animal or pet in the space beside Rapunzel.

27

Escape The Tower Game

Rapunzel dreams of exploring the world outside her tower. Can you help her break out? There's only one problem ... Mother Gothel will try and stop you every step of the way.
Let's play Escape the Tower!

You will need:
Counters (coins, paper or toy figures)
A dice
2-4 players

How to play:
* Place your counters on the START and take turns to roll the dice.
* Move forward the number of spaces rolled.
* If you land on Rapunzel, climb up her hair.
* If you land on Mother Gothel, slide down the black rope.
* The first one to reach the castle is the winner!

Adventurous Moana

Best friend ...
Pua.

Likes ...
to sail across the ocean.

Dislikes ...
being told she can't go in the ocean!

Princess power ...
Moana saved the island of Motunui.

Moana's story ...
Ever since she can remember, the ocean has called to Moana, but her father will not let her go past the reef. When her island home of Motunui is in danger, the ocean calls once more. This time Moana listens, and she sets sail on the voyage of a lifetime to find the secrets of the past.

The ocean chose me!

Maui Mission

Maui wants to relax today, but Moana is determined to take him on a mission to find Te Fiti. Help Moana battle past the Kakamora to Te Fiti.

Follow this pattern to find the way.

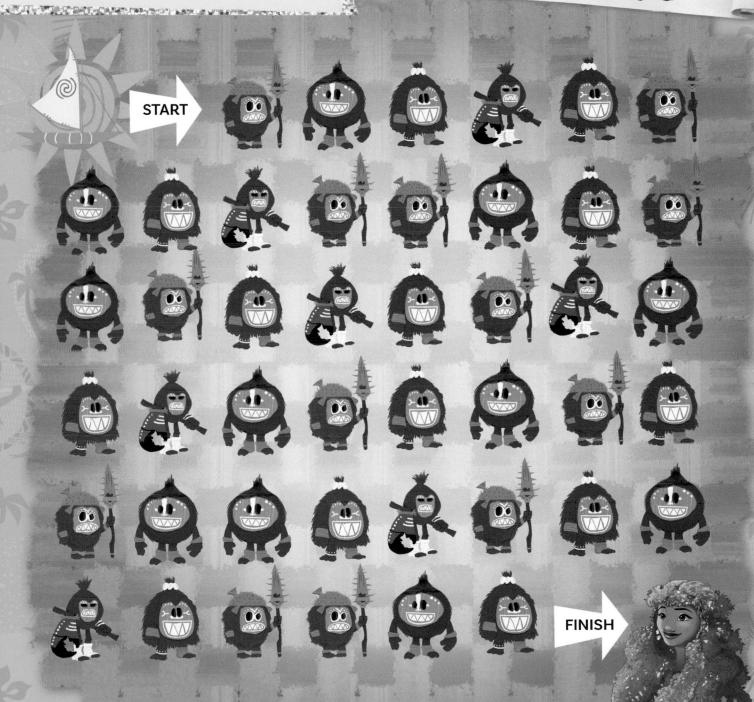

START

FINISH

Answer on page 69.

A Helping Hand

"Shoo!"

1 Moana, her pet pig Pua, and the village rooster, Heihei, were helping the villagers harvest coconuts. But silly Heihei was getting in everyone's way!

1 Write down how many coconuts the villagers have harvested so far.

Answer on page 69.

2 Heihei pecked at a coconut husk and got a piece stuck on his beak. It covered his eyes so he couldn't see where he was going. "Careful!" Moana cried, as Heihei ran towards the tree.

3 But before Moana could stop him, Heihei crashed into the trunk. The tree wobbled and a coconut fell, landing with a bump on Pua's head. The poor pig ran away in fright.

It's OK, Pua.

We love coconuts!

4 Moana found her friend on the beach and told him not to fear coconuts. She explained how important they were to the island, just like Gramma Tala had told her when she was younger.

5 But the frightened pig wouldn't go back to the coconut grove. So Moana decided to show Pua all the great things about coconuts.

Come in!

Try it!

Come closer!

6 "We use the fibres to make fishing nets, eat the flesh and use the leaves to make fires," she said gently. But Pua was still too frightened to go back to the coconut grove.

2 Spot these close-ups in the pictures above.

 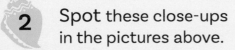  

I need an idea.

"You can't live on Motunui and be scared of the coconut grove!" Moana sighed. "I need to think of a way to make them fun for Pua." Just then, Gramma Tala walked by, trailing a stick in the sand.

8

"You have the answer," she told Moana, wisely, "you just need to look at what you've got." Gramma Tala dug the stick into the sand in front of Moana and left her alone.

3 **Follow** the trail Gramma Tala has made in the sand.

Gramma Tala was right!

9

Moana was wondering what Gramma Tala meant when the coconut she was holding rolled out of her hand. It crashed into the stick Gramma Tala had left, knocking it down. Moana had an idea.

10 Moana quickly set up a row of sticks in the sand and went to find Pua. She showed her friend how to roll a coconut to try and knock the sticks down. Pua couldn't wait to have a go!

11

Soon, Moana and Pua's squeals of delight drew the other villagers to the beach. Moana had helped Pua overcome his fear of the coconut grove and had invented a fun game for everyone to enjoy.

Start

The End

4 Find these villagers in the picture.

5 Draw Pua playing with a coconut.

Ocean Dreams

Moana dreams of sailing away on the big, blue sea. Draw over the lines to build her a boat so she can start her ocean adventure.

Add fun colours and patterns to your boat. Here are some ideas:

Make A Splash!

Pua and Moana love jumping in the ocean waves. Which one of these pictures is different to the rest?

1

2

4

3

Shout out **'SPLASH!'** when you spot the odd one out!

Answer on page 69.

37

Bold Jasmine

Best friend ...
Rajah.

Likes ...
being free and seeing new things.

Dislikes ...
being stuck in her palace bedroom.

Princess power ...
Jasmine wears a disguise, so nobody knows she is a princess.

Jasmine's story ...
Life inside the palace is full of luxury, but Jasmine wants more from life. Staying there all the time can be boring, boring, boring! One day, she sneaks outside and meets a new friend, Aladdin. Together, they set off on a sky-high mission and discover a whole new world. Life will never be boring again ...

It's a magical world!

Suns Vs Moons

As the sun goes down, Jasmine wants to explore outside. Rajah wants to wait until the morning. Let's play Suns Vs Moons to decide who wins.

Draw a sun like this:

Draw a moon like this:

Best out of three!

How to Play:

- One player is Rajah and draws suns.
- One player is Jasmine and draws moons.
- Take turns to draw a sun or a moon in each square.
- The first person to get three of the same images in a row across, down or diagonally, is the winner.

GAME 1

GAME 2

GAME 3

A Whole New World

Jasmine is ready for a big adventure. Guide her through the clouds on the Magic Carpet to pick up Aladdin.

START

FINISH

41

Monkey Mischief

Genie and Abu are playing tricks. Can you spot the matching pair of pictures?

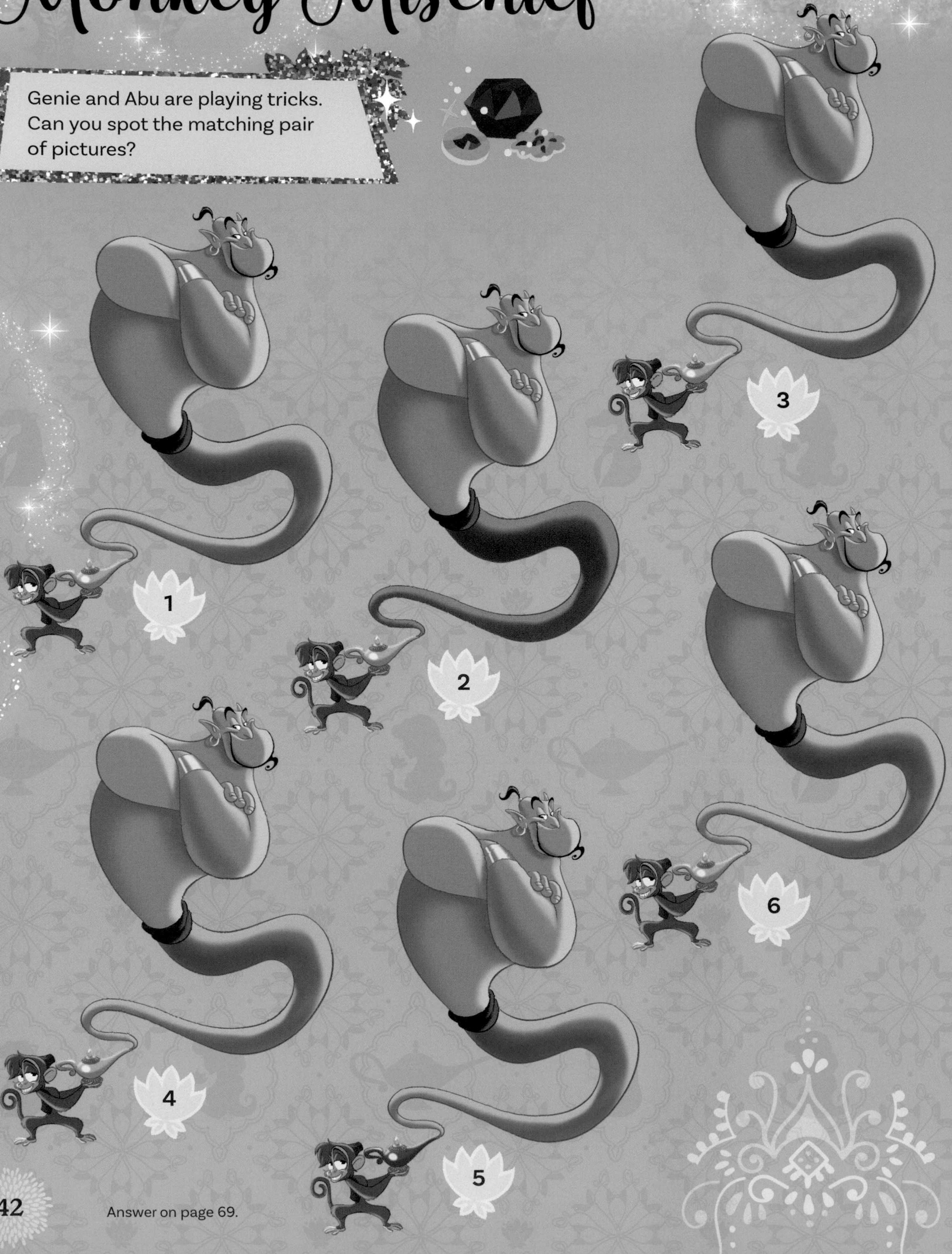

1

2

3

4

5

6

Answer on page 69.

Magic Trails

43

Sshh ... Quietly trace a pencil to guide Jasmine to the magic lamp. If you crash into the sides, Jafar and Iago might see you and you will have to start again!

FINISH →

← START

Talented Tiana

Best friend ...
Charlotte Le Bouff.

Likes ...
cooking for
her friends.

Hobbies ...
playing music
and dancing.

Princess power ...
Tiana worked hard
every day to open her
own restaurant.

Tiana's story ...
Nothing is impossible for Tiana!
When she wants to open her own
restaurant, she is determined to
make it happen, even when others
don't believe in her. Sometimes
she can work a little too hard. It's
not until she turns into a frog, that
she finds there is magic in love and
friendship too.

*Make
your own
destiny!*

Memory Game

Get your feet tapping and let the music begin!
Look at this party picture carefully. Then cover it up
with some paper and test your memory.

1. Is Charlotte wearing a hat?
2. What little animal is singing along?
3. How many alligators are there?
4. What colour is Tiana's dress?

Answers on page 69.

Tiana's Big Dream

1 Ever since she was a little girl, Tiana had loved to cook. She spent hours in the kitchen with her father cooking pots of gumbo and dreaming of the restaurant she'd own one day.

Mmmmm, perfect!

1 Trace the trail to stir the gumbo.

2 When she was older, Tiana got a job as a waitress. She saved every spare penny she earned but she still didn't have enough to buy a restaurant. "I need a second job," Tiana thought.

3 So Tiana asked Mrs Johnson at the dress shop. "You sew well," Mrs Johnson told her, "but I'm afraid I'm not hiring anyone until Mardi Gras." "I'll check back then," sighed Tiana.

You've got your mother's gift.

4 Tiana's next stop was the hardware store. "Have you got any jobs?" she asked as she grabbed a hammer to fix a loose sign. "I'm sorry, I've just hired my nephew," replied the owner.

2 Point to the items that belong in the hardware shop.

Thank you for your BUSINESS

That's better.

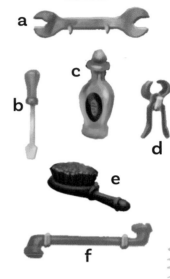

a

b

c

d

e

f

Answers on page 69.

5 Then she asked at Cora's beauty parlour. "Show me what you can do," said Cora. But Tiana's hairstyle looked more like a wedding cake! "I guess it's not for me," she sighed.

Oh my!

Ta-dah!

6 Tiana's spirits were drooping so she went to Duke's Café for a rest. Buford the chef gave her a doughnut to cheer her up. "I guarantee it will put a smile on your face," he said.

Don't be down.

7 Back at home Tiana decided to bake a batch of beignets for Buford to say thank you for being so kind.

These are to say 'thank you'.

8

She delivered the tray of beignets to Buford straightaway. Their scrumptious scent wafted all around the café. "Can I try one?" asked a customer. "Me too!" said another. "And me!"

9 Word soon spread about Tiana's tasty treats and a long queue formed outside Duke's Café. But there weren't enough beignets for everyone. "Can you bake some more?" Buford asked.

We need more beignets!

No problem!

3 Spot these hungry customers in the queue.

10 In no time at all Tiana whipped up a big batch of beignets for everyone to enjoy and Burford offered her a job as a beignet cook. She was one step closer to her dream.

The End

Menu

4 **Write** how many coins Tiana has earned.

Answer on page 69.

5 **Draw** your favourite tasty treat here.

Brave Mulan

Best friend ...
Mushu.

Likes ...
hanging out with her family and pets.

Hobbies ...
riding her family horse, Khan.

Princess power ...
Mulan is a hero warrior who wins battles.

Mulan's story ...
When her sick, old father is told to fight in the army, Mulan has a brave plan. By cutting off her hair and dressing up as a man, she joins the army in her father's place. She soon proves to everyone what a strong fighter she is. Nobody is a match for mighty Mulan!

Be your own hero!

Warrior Words

There is nothing Mulan won't do to protect her family. She is the ultimate warrior. Use a pencil to trace over these words all about Mulan.

brave

kind

strong

hero

Light Up The World

Answer on page 69.

Mulan is getting ready for a party with her family.
How many glowing lanterns can you count?

I can count [ ] lanterns.

Can you spot
Mushu hiding
on the page?

52

Power Puzzle

Mulan is rounding up her friends and family for a surprise picnic. Can you find three-in-a-row of each guest?

Write how many times each guest appears on the grid. Which appears the most?

Answers on page 69.

Smart Cinderella

Best friend ...
Bruno, her pet dog.

Dreams ...
Finding happiness outside her home.

Hobbies ...
Making clothes for her mice friends.

Princess power ...
Cinderella has the strength to stay happy even when life is hard.

Cinderella's story ...
Every day, Cinderella's stepmother makes her clean, cook and scrub until their home is sparkling. Life is tough, until everything changes one magical day. In a sprinkle of sparkles, the Fairy Godmother casts a spell and whisks Cinderella off to a ball. All of Cinderella's dreams are about to come true!

Stepping into my dreams!

Adventure Ready!

Grab your crayons and get Cinderella ready for a fun adventure. Copy the colours to help you.

Where do you think Cinderella is going? Talk about her adventure!

Cinderella's Surprise

1 Cinderella was excited because a travelling salesman was visiting the palace that day. "I'll choose some new goblets as a present for the Prince," she thought happily.

I can't wait for the salesman to arrive.

2 While Cinderella was waiting for the salesman to arrive, the sky turned grey and there was a huge downpour of rain. "I hope he's OK," she said to Gus and Jaq.

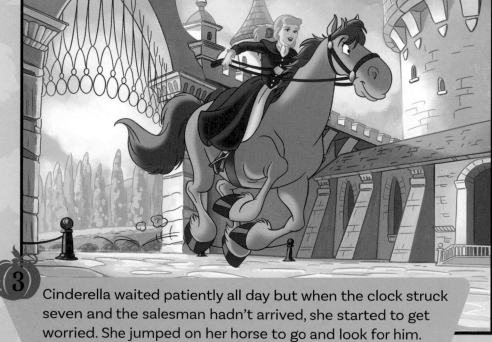

3 Cinderella waited patiently all day but when the clock struck seven and the salesman hadn't arrived, she started to get worried. She jumped on her horse to go and look for him.

1 Trace over the clock hands.

4 After a while, Cinderella spotted the salesman. His horse was refusing to cross a huge muddy puddle and there was no other way around. "I think I can help," Cinderella called.

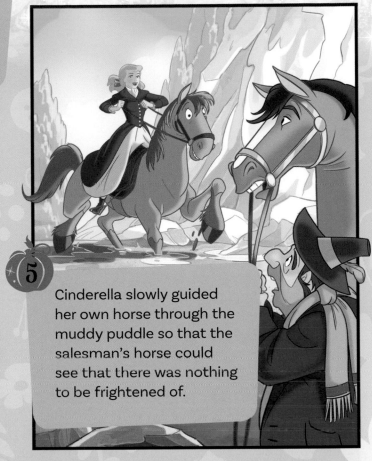

5 Cinderella slowly guided her own horse through the muddy puddle so that the salesman's horse could see that there was nothing to be frightened of.

 **6** "Now it's your turn," said Cinderella. The salesman encouraged his horse to go through the puddle and this time it did. "I hank you so much!" the salesman cried happily.

 **2** Circle what you think is the best thing to wash the muddy horse with.

Sponge, soap and water

Toothbrush

Answer on page 69.

7 Then the salesman shone a lamp in his wagon so that Cinderella could have a look through his wares. "These are perfect," she said, choosing a set of colourful, glass goblets.

8 But one of the goblets was broken. "It must have broken when the horse suddenly stopped at the puddle," the salesman told her. "Don't worry," replied Cinderella. "I have an idea."

The prince will love them!

Oh dear!

3 Spot these items in the picture above.

a

b

c

d

9 Back at the palace, Cinderella smashed the broken goblet into pieces and filed the edges to make them smooth. Then she stuck the pieces on to the remaining goblets to decorate them.

58

10 The next morning the Prince was overjoyed when Cinderella gave him her present. "Where did you find such unusual goblets?" he asked.

11 "It was all thanks to lots of rain, a muddy puddle and my helpful horse," Cinderella told the confused Prince with a smile.

The End

4 Tick what the prince is having for breakfast.

a

b

5 Decorate this goblet for Cinderella.

Answers on page 69.

59

All About ...
Kind Aurora

Lives ...
in the forest with
the three good fairies.

Likes ...
dancing with her
animal friends.

Dreams ...
of finding happiness
and true love.

Princess power ...
Aurora has the power of
kindness.

Aurora's story ...
Although she is a true princess, Aurora was brought up by the three good fairies far from her castle home. An evil curse was cast upon her as a baby, and she was sent away to hide. Aurora is happy in her peaceful life ... until she learns the truth and it's time to come face to face with her curse.

Dreams do come true!

You Grow Girl

Aurora's forest flowers are ready to bloom. Colour the sun, raindrops and flowers. Then add more raindrops to help the flowers grow **bigger** and **bigger!**

Caring Snow White

Best friends ...
Sleepy, Doc, Bashful, Dopey, Grumpy, Sleepy, Sneezy.

Likes ...
singing to her animal friends.

Dislikes ...
being grumpy. She can even make Grumpy smile!

Princess power ...
She helps people see the good in the world.

Snow White's story ...
Snow White's life changes forever when her wicked stepmother forces her to run away. Alone and lost, she soon makes friends with the Seven Dwarves and sets up a new happy home. All is well, until her stepmother poisons her with an apple. Can true love and friendship save Snow White from the evil curse?

Be a friend you can trust.

Forest Friends

Snow White loves all the creatures in the forest, and they love her too! Trace over the letters with a pencil and draw lines to match each word to the right animal.

hen

snail

bird

frog

deer

Answers on page 69.

Let's Get Active

Roll a dice and try out the fun princess activity on the matching number square. Keep rolling until you have done them all.

1 Sing a song with *Belle*.

2 Twirl around with *Cinderella*.

3 Do a dance with *Tiana*.

4 Practise warrior moves with *Mulan*.

5 Leap in the air with *Jasmine*.

6 Paint a picture with *Rapunzel*.

Follow your Dreams!

Quiz Quest

How much do you know about the princesses and their worlds? Take the quiz to find out! Circle your answers.

1. Who is *Ariel's* best friend?

   a) Flounder
   b) Ursula

2. What does *Tiana* turn into?

   a) a frog
   b) an alligator

3. What does *Belle* love to do best?

   a) play the piano
   b) read books

4. Where is *Moana* the happiest?
   a) on land

   b) in the ocean

5. Who lives with *Rapunzel* in the tower?
   a) Pascal

   b) Flynn Ryder

6. What or who poisons *Snow White*?
   a) an apple
   b) Grumpy

7. How does *Cinderella* get to the ball?
   a) on a ship
   b) in a magic carriage

8. Which *princess* is known as a fierce warrior?

   a) Mulan
   b) Jasmine

Answers on page 69.

Be A Hero

Being kind, brave, caring and true is what makes the princesses the ultimate heroes. Use bright and bold colours to decorate this power poster.